STATE OF WASHINGTON ET AL
V.
UNITED STATES FOOD AND DRUG ADMINISTRATION ET AL.

THOMAS O. RICE
UNITED STATES DISTRICT JUDGE
UNITED STATES DISTRICT COURT
EASTERN DISTRICT OF WASHINGTON

FOREWORD BY CINCINNATUS [AI]
ENHANCED BY NIMBLE BOOKS AI

PUBLISHING INFORMATION

(c) 2023 Nimble Books LLC

ISBN: 978-0-9799205-6-1

AI Lab for Book-Lovers No. 24

Humans and AI making books richer, more diverse, and more surprising.

BIBLIOGRAPHIC KEYWORDS
AI-GENERATED KEYWORD PHRASES

Court order; Preliminary injunction; U.S. Food and Drug Administration; Mifepristone; Medication abortion; United States District Judge; Thomas O. Rice; Eastern District of the United States; Risk Evaluation and Mitigation Strategy; REMS; Distribution restrictions; Administration restrictions; COVID-19 pandemic; Patients; Healthcare providers; Administrative Procedure Act; Economic costs; Irreparable harm; In-person dispensing requirement; Amicus curiae brief; Third party; Legal decision; Access to

FOREWORD

Access to safe and legal abortion is a crucial aspect of reproductive healthcare for people all around the world. However, in recent years we have seen attacks on this fundamental right, with restrictions and barriers placed on those seeking abortion care. And now, after a global pandemic, these barriers have become even more pronounced.

In this decision, a US District Judge brings his expertise and experience to bear on the topic of medication abortion regulation in the United States. As this court order demonstrates, the regulations surrounding medication abortion are complex and controversial - but they also have real-world impacts on patients seeking care.

The judiciary, exeutive, and legislative branches of the US government have spent years studying these issues from every possible angle: medical, legal, ethical, and social. Their insights into how medication abortion is regulated in practice are reflected in the current state of the law.

But more than that – this decision isn't just about understanding why the right of access to medication abortions is so important; it's also about taking action to make sure that people can actually receive that care when they need it most. As we continue to grapple with the ongoing COVID-19 pandemic - not to mention persistent efforts by anti-choice forces to chip away at reproductive rights – decisions, and actions, like this one are needed now more than ever.

So whether you're a healthcare provider who wants to know how best help your patients navigate complicated regulatory systems or an activist looking for ways to fight back against unjust restrictions on access to care - I highly recommend reading this insightful decision. By shedding light on these critical issues surrounding access reproductive health services , Judge Rice offers us both insight into our current situation as well as hope for a better future where everyone has control over their bodies and choices.

Cincinnatus [AI]

ABSTRACTS

TL;DR (ONE WORD)

Injunction.

TL;DR (VANILLA)

A court order grants a preliminary injunction in part against the FDA's current REMS program for mifepristone, which includes restrictions on distribution and administration. The injunction enjoins the FDA from enforcing the in-person dispensing requirement for mifepristone during the COVID-19 pandemic and maintains the status quo of the current REMS program until a determination on the merits. A third party's motion for leave to file an amicus curiae brief is denied.

EXPLAIN IT TO ME LIKE I'M FIVE YEARS OLD

This is a paper from a judge telling the people who make rules about medicine (called the FDA) to change some of their rules for a medicine called mifepristone. This medicine helps people have abortions. The judge thinks that the rules the FDA made are too hard for people and doctors to follow, especially during the COVID-19 pandemic. The judge says that the FDA can't make people go in person to get the medicine right now, but they can keep the other rules until they make

ACTION ITEMS

Advocate for the full granting of the preliminary injunction to ensure that patients and healthcare providers have access to medication abortion during the COVID-19 pandemic without unnecessary restrictions.

Monitor the progress of this case and other legal challenges to restrictions on medication abortion and advocate for policies that prioritize patient-centered care and access to abortion.

SCIENTIFIC STYLE

A court order issued by United States District Judge Thomas O. Rice in the Eastern District of the United States on April 7, 2023 grants a preliminary injunction in part against the FDA's current Risk Evaluation and Mitigation Strategy (REMS) for mifepristone, a medication used for medication abortion. The court finds that the alleged unrecoverable economic costs in this case are sufficient to demonstrate irreparable harm and enjoin the FDA from enforcing the in-person dispensing requirement for mifepristone during the COVID-19 pandemic. The court also denies a third party's unopposed motion for leave to file an amicus curiae brief, finding it not particularly helpful to the court's findings on the present motion.

VIEWPOINTS

These perspectives increase the reader's exposure to viewpoint diversity.

FORMAL DISSENT

A member of the organization responsible for this document may have principled, substantive reasons to dissent from this report. One possible reason could be a belief that the court order undermines the FDA's ability to regulate medication abortion in a safe and effective manner. This member may argue that the REMS program is necessary to protect patient safety and that the court's decision to enjoin the in-person dispensing requirement during the pandemic may increase the risk of adverse events or complications associated with medication abortion.

Another possible reason for dissent could be a concern about the economic impact of the preliminary injunction. This member may believe that the alleged unrecoverable economic costs cited by the plaintiffs are overstated or do not outweigh the potential benefits of the REMS program. They may argue that the court's decision to maintain the status quo of the current REMS program until a determination on the merits is made is insufficient to address these concerns.

Finally, this member may disagree with the court's decision to deny the third party's motion for leave to file an amicus curiae brief. They may believe that the proposed brief could have provided valuable legal or substantive information that would have been helpful to the court's findings on the present motion. They may argue that the court's decision to delay consideration of the brief until a trial on the merits is unnecessary and could lead to further delays or complications in resolving the case.

RED TEAM CRITIQUE

In the case of the court order granting a preliminary injunction against the FDA's REMS program for mifepristone, a red team critique might focus on the potential risks to public health posed by loosening the restrictions on distribution and administration of the medication. The critique might also explore the legal basis for the plaintiffs' claims under the APA and argue that they do not meet the legal standard for a preliminary injunction. Additionally, the critique might explore alternative ways to ensure access to medication abortions during the pandemic that do not compromise the safety of patients.

MAGA Perspective

This court order is a prime example of liberal judges trying to push their pro-abortion agenda. The FDA has every right to regulate the distribution and administration of medication abortions, especially during a pandemic when we need to prioritize public health and safety. These plaintiffs are just trying to make it easier for women to kill their unborn babies and ignore any potential risks or complications.

The fact that the court is even considering granting an injunction against the in-person dispensing requirement shows a complete lack of concern for the well-being of patients. How can we trust healthcare providers to properly administer this medication without proper supervision? This decision puts lives at risk and ignores the fact that medication abortions have been proven to have serious side effects and complications, including hemorrhage and incomplete abortion.

Furthermore, the denial of the third party's motion for leave to file an amicus curiae brief is a blatant disregard for the importance of outside voices in legal cases. It's clear that this court is only interested in pushing their own agenda and silencing any opposition. We need to stand up against this type of judicial activism and protect the lives of unborn babies and their mothers.

In the end, this court order is nothing more than an attack on traditional values and the sanctity of human life. We must continue to fight back against these dangerous decisions and uphold the important work of the FDA in regulating medication abortions.

SUMMARIES

METHODS

Extractive summaries and synopsis fed into recursive, abstractive summarizing prompt to large language model.

Reduced word count from 6899 to 23 words by extracting the 20 most significant sentences, then looping through that collection in chunks of 2500 tokens for 2 rounds until the number of words in the remaining text fits between the target floor and ceiling. Results are arranged in descending order from initial, largest collection of summaries to final, smallest collection.

Machine-generated and unsupervised; use with caution.

RECURSIVE SUMMARY ROUND 0

Plaintiffs' motion for preliminary injunction partially granted in case 1:23-cv-03026-TOR. Third parties' unopposed motion for leave to file amicus brief also granted. Preliminary injunction can be either prohibitory or mandatory. Likelihood of success on the merits considered.

The court granted the plaintiff's motion for preliminary injunction in part, determining that the APA alone does not demonstrate congressional intent to authorize a state to sue the federal government as parens patriae. Administrative exhaustion is necessary to obtain injunctive relief, and the court must uphold agency action unless there are serious questions going to the merits of the claims or it is likely to succeed on the merits.

Plaintiffs argue that the decision relied on factors Congress did not intend to consider and failed to consider an important aspect. Defendants argue plaintiffs fail to show irreparable harm due to loosened restrictions and delayed filing. Preliminary injunction granted until January 2023.

Defendants are preliminarily enjoined from altering the status or rights of parties under the Mifepristone REMS program until a determination on the merits is made.

Recursive Summary Round 1

Partial preliminary injunction granted in case, administrative exhaustion necessary for injunctive relief, defendants enjoined from altering Mifepristone REMS program until merits are determined.

Virtual Context Summary

Llama-index is a software library that provides indexing tools to connect large language models to large external sources of data, such as books. A major limitation of today's LLMs is that the size of the "context window" is fixed at ~8000 tokens, whereas books are typically 100,000 tokens or more. Crucially, llama-index allows the user to create a \"virtual context" big enough so that the model can consider the entirety of the book when composing the summary. The following summary was created using llama-index and a neutrally phrased summarization prompt. Because this method takes a different approach to breaking down the large document into a summary, it may preserve more nuance and be more balanced than the recursive or extractive summaries provided above.

This document is a court order granting in part a preliminary injunction sought by plaintiffs against the U.S. Food and Drug Administration (FDA) regarding the regulation of mifepristone, a medication used for medication abortion. The court order was issued by United States District Judge Thomas O. Rice in the Eastern District of the United States on April 7, 2023. The plaintiffs argue that the FDA's current Risk Evaluation and Mitigation Strategy (REMS) for mifepristone, which includes restrictions on distribution and administration, is unnecessary and imposes undue burdens on patients and healthcare providers, particularly during the COVID-19 pandemic. The court finds that there are serious issues going to the merits of the plaintiffs' claims under the Administrative Procedure Act (APA) and that the alleged unrecoverable economic costs in this case are sufficient to demonstrate irreparable harm. The court grants the preliminary injunction in part, enjoining the FDA from enforcing the in-person dispensing requirement for mifepristone during the COVID-19 pandemic and maintaining the status quo of the current REMS program until a determination on the merits.

The court order also denied a third party's unopposed motion for leave to file an amicus curiae brief, noting that the proposed brief offered no additional legal or substantive information that was particularly helpful to the court's findings on the present motion. The court stated that the brief may be more useful during a trial on the merits. The court directed the District Court Executive to enter the order and furnish copies to counsel. No bond shall be required pursuant to Federal Rule of Civil Procedure 65(c).

Overall, this document represents a legal decision in a case involving access to medication abortions during the COVID-19 pandemic. The court order grants a preliminary injunction in part against the FDA's current REMS program for mifepristone and denies a third party's motion for leave to file an amicus curiae brief.

1

2

3

4

5   UNITED STATES DISTRICT COURT

6   EASTERN DISTRICT OF WASHINGTON

7 | STATE OF WASHINGTON, STATE
    | OF OREGON, STATE OF ARIZONA,   NO. 1:23-CV-3026-TOR
8 | STATE OF COLORADO, STATE OF
    | CONNECTICUT, STATE OF   ORDER GRANTING IN PART
9 | DELAWARE, STATE OF ILLINOIS,   PLAINTIFFS' MOTION FOR
    | ATTORNEY GENERAL OF   PRELIMINARY INJUNCTION
10 | MICHIGAN, STATE OF NEVADA,
    | STATE OF NEW MEXICO, STATE
11 | OF RHODE ISLAND, STATE OF
    | VERMONT, DISTRICT OF
12 | COLUMBIA, STATE OF HAWAII,
    | STATE OF MAINE, STATE OF
13 | MARYLAND, STATE OF
    | MINNESOTA, and
14 | COMMONWEALTH OF
    | PENNSYVLANIA,

15

               Plaintiffs,

16

       v.

17

    UNITED STATES FOOD AND
18 DRUG ADMINISTRATION,
    ROBERT M. CALIFF, in his official
19 capacity as Commissioner of Food and
    Drugs, UNITED STATES
20 DEPARTMENT OF HEALTH AND
    HUMAN SERVICES, and XAVIER

ORDER GRANTING IN PART PLAINTIFFS' MOTION FOR
PRELIMINARY INJUNCTION ~ 1

1 BECERRA, in his official capacity as
   Secretary of the Department of Health
2 and Human Services,

3   Defendants.

4   BEFORE THE COURT are Plaintiffs' Motion for Preliminary Injunction

5   (ECF No. 3), Third Parties' Unopposed Motion for Leave to File Amicus Curiae

6   Brief (ECF No. 52), and Third Parties' Unopposed Motion for Leave to File

7   Amicus Brief (ECF No. 69). The Motion for Preliminary Injunction was submitted

8   for consideration with oral argument on March 28, 2023. Kristin Beneski, Colleen

9   M. Melody, and Noah G. Purcell appeared on behalf of Plaintiffs. Noah T. Katzen,

10 Aravind Sreenath, and Molly Smith appeared on behalf of Defendants. The Court

11 has reviewed the record and files herein, and is fully informed. For the reasons

12 discussed below, Plaintiffs' Motion for Preliminary Injunction (ECF No. 3) is

13 **granted in part**, Third Parties' Unopposed Motion for Leave to File Amicus

14 Curiae Brief (ECF No. 52) is **denied**, and Third Parties' Unopposed Motion for

15 Leave to File Amicus Brief (ECF No. 69) is **denied**.

16   **BACKGROUND**

17   This case concerns federal regulation of mifepristone used in connection

18 with the termination of early pregnancy. ECF No. 35. Plaintiffs seek a

19 preliminary injunction, asking this Court to "affirm[] "FDA's original conclusion

20 that mifepristone is safe and effective, preserv[e] the status quo by enjoining any

1 │ actions by Defendants to remove this critical drug from the market, and enjoin[]

2 │ the unnecessary and burdensome January 2023 restrictions." ECF No. 3 at 5. The

3 │ parties timely filed their respective response and reply. ECF Nos. 51, 60. The

4 │ following facts are generally undisputed for purposes of resolving the instant

5 │ motion.

6 │   In 1992, Subpart H regulations authorized the Food and Drug

7 │ Administration ("FDA") to require conditions "needed to assure safe use" for

8 │ certain drugs. Final Rule, 57 Fed. Reg. 58,942, 58,958 (December 11, 1992)

9 │ (codified at 21 C.FR. § 314.520). In September 2000, FDA approved

10 │ mifepristone[1] under Subpart H, concluding that mifepristone is safe and effective

11 │ for medical termination of intrauterine pregnancy through 49 days' gestation when

12 │ used in a regimen with the already-approved drug, misoprostol. ECF No. 35 at 21,

13 │ ¶ 85. FDA's restrictions on mifepristone included requiring (1) an in-person

14 │ dispensing requirement where the drug could only be dispensed in a hospital,

15 │ clinic, or medical office, by or under the supervision of a certified provider who at

16 │ the time could only be a physician, (2) providers attest to their clinical abilities in a

17 │

_____

18 │ [1]   As referenced herein, mifepristone is the drug used for early termination of

19 │ pregnancy, such as Mifeprex and the generic drug. This Order does not impact

20 │ mifepristone as used in Korlym, a drug used to treat Cushing's syndrome.

ORDER GRANTING IN PART PLAINTIFFS' MOTION FOR
PRELIMINARY INJUNCTION ~ 3

1   signed form kept on file by the manufacturer, and agree to comply with reporting

2   and other REMS requirements, and (3) prescribers and patients review and sign a

3   form with information about the regimen and risks and that the prescriber provide

4   copies to the patient and patient's medical record. *Id.* at 24, ¶ 87.

5   From 1992 to February 2002, seven New Drug Applications ("NDA"),

6   including Mifeprex, were approved subject to these conditions, in contrast to the

7   961 NDAs with no additional restrictions from January 1993 to September 2005.

8   ECF No. 35 at 24–25, ¶ 88.

9   The Food and Drug Administration Amendments Act of 2007 effectively

10   replaced Subpart H with the REMS statute codified at 21 U.S.C. § 355-1. Pub. L.

11   No. 110-85, tit. IX, § 901. All drugs previously approved under Subpart H,

12   including Mifeprex, were deemed to have a REMS in place. Pub. L. No. 110-85,

13   tit. IX, § 909(b). Under the Federal Food, Drug and Cosmetic Act ("FDCA"), a

14   new drug cannot be marketed and prescribed until it undergoes a rigorous approval

15   process to determine that it is safe and effective. 21 U.S.C. § 355.

16   In 2011, FDA issued a new REMS for Mifeprex incorporating the same

17   restrictions under which the drug was approved eleven years earlier. *Id.*, ¶ 90; ECF

18   No. 51-2. In 2013, FDA reviewed the existing REMS and reaffirmed the

19   restrictions in place. ECF No. 35 at 25, ¶ 91.

20

ORDER GRANTING IN PART PLAINTIFFS' MOTION FOR
PRELIMINARY INJUNCTION ~ 4

1   In 2015, Mifeprex's manufacturer submitted a supplemental NDA proposing

2   to update the label to reflect evidence-based practices across the country – namely,

3   the use of 200 mg of mifepristone instead of 600 mg. *Id.*, ¶ 92. In July 2015, the

4   manufacturer submitted its REMS assessment, proposing minor modifications. *Id.*

5   This submission prompted a review of the Mifeprex label and REMS by FDA. *Id.*

6   at 26, ¶ 93. As part of the review, FDA received letters from more than 40 medical

7   experts, researches, advocacy groups, and professional associations who asked,

8   *inter alia*, that the REMS be eliminated in their entirety. *Id.* One letter asked FDA

9   to "[e]liminate the REMS and ETASU (Elements to Assure Safe Use), including

10   eliminating the certification and patient agreement requirements. *Id.* at 27, ¶ 95.

11   In 2016, FDA found "no new safety concerns have arisen in recent years,

12   and that the known serious risks occur rarely," and that "[g]iven that the number of

13   … adverse events appear to be stable or decreased over time, it is likely that …

14   serious adverse events will remain acceptably low." *Id.* at 30, ¶ 100. Following

15   this review, FDA changed Mifeprex's indication, labeling, and REMS, including

16   increasing the gestational age limit from 49 to 70 days, reducing the number of

17   required in-person clinic visits to one, finding at-home administration of

18   misoprostol safe, finding no significant differences in outcomes based on whether

19   patients had a follow-up phone call or in person or based on the timing of those

20   appointments, and allowing a broader set of healthcare providers to prescribe

1   mifepristone. *Id.*, ¶ 101. However, FDA still required that mifepristone be

2   administered in a clinic setting. *Id.*

3   In 2019, FDA approved a different manufacturer's abbreviated NDA for a

4   generic version of mifepristone and established the Mifepristone REMS Program,

5   which covered both Mifeprex and the generic drug. *Id.* at 32, ¶ 103; ECF No. 51-

6   3. In May 2020, American College of Obstetricians and Gynecologists ("ACOG")

7   sued FDA, challenging the Mifepristone REMS Program's in-person dispensing

8   requirement in light of the COVID-19 pandemic. ECF No. 35, ¶ 104.   In that

9   case, the district court temporarily enjoined FDA from enforcing the in-person

10   dispensation requirements under the REMS in light of the COVID-19 pandemic.

11   *American College of Obstetricians and Gynecologists v. United States Food and*

12   *Drug Administration*, 47 2F. Supp. 3d 183 (D. Md. 2020).

13   In April 2021, FDA suspended the in-person dispensing requirement during

14   the COVID-19 public health emergency because, during the six-month period in

15   which the in-person dispensing requirement had been enjoined, the availability of

16   mifepristone by mail showed no increases in serious patient safety concerns. *Id.*, ¶

17   105.

18   On May 7, 2021, FDA announced it would review whether the Mifepristone

19   REMS Program should be modified. ECF No. 51-4. FDA reviewed materials

20   between March 29, 2016 and July 26, 2021, as well as publications found on

ORDER GRANTING IN PART PLAINTIFFS' MOTION FOR
PRELIMINARY INJUNCTION ~ 6

1   PubMed and Embase and those provided by "advocacy groups, individuals,

2   plaintiffs in *Chelius v. Becerra*, 1:17-493-JAO-RT (D. Haw.), application holders,

3   and healthcare providers and researchers. *Id.* at 10–11.

4   On December 16, 2021, FDA announced its conclusions regarding the

5   Mifepristone REMS Program. ECF No. 51-5. On January 3, 2023, FDA accepted

6   these conclusions by approving the supplemental applications proposing

7   conforming modifications. ECF Nos. 51-8; 51-11. The 2023 REMS removed the

8   in-person dispensing requirement and added a pharmacy-certification requirement.

9   ECF Nos. 51-4, 51-5. The FDA maintained the Prescriber and Patient Agreement

10   Form requirements. *Id.*

11   **DISCUSSION**

12   **I.   Preliminary Injunction Standard**

13   Plaintiffs, on behalf of themselves and as *parens patriae* in protecting the

14   health and well-being of its residents, moves for a preliminary injunction

15   "affirming FDA's original conclusion that mifepristone is safe and effective,

16   preserving the status quo by enjoining any actions by Defendants to remove this

17   critical drug from the market, and enjoining the unnecessary and burdensome

18   January 2023 restrictions." *See* ECF Nos. 3 at 5; 35.

19   Pursuant to Federal Rule of Civil Procedure 65, the Court may grant

20   preliminary injunctive relief in order to prevent "immediate and irreparable

1 injury." Fed. R. Civ. P. 65(b)(1)(A). To obtain this relief, a plaintiff must

2 demonstrate: (1) a likelihood of success on the merits; (2) a likelihood of

3 irreparable injury in the absence of preliminary relief; (3) that a balancing of the

4 hardships weighs in plaintiff's favor; and (4) that a preliminary injunction will

5 advance the public interest. *Winter v. Nat. Res. Def. Council, Inc.*, 555 U.S. 7, 20

6 (2008); *M.R. v. Dreyfus*, 697 F.3d 706, 725 (9th Cir. 2012). Under the *Winter* test,

7 a plaintiff must satisfy each element for injunctive relief.

8   Alternatively, the Ninth Circuit also permits a "sliding scale" approach

9 under which an injunction may be issued if there are "serious questions going to

10 the merits" and "the balance of hardships tips sharply in the plaintiff's favor,"

11 assuming the plaintiff also satisfies the two other *Winter* factors. *All. for the Wild*

12 *Rockies v. Cottrell*, 632 F.3d 1127, 1131 (9th Cir. 2011) ("[A] stronger showing of

13 one element may offset a weaker showing of another."); *see also Farris v.*

14 *Seabrook*, 677 F.3d 858, 864 (9th Cir. 2012) ("We have also articulated an

15 alternate formulation of the *Winter* test, under which serious questions going to the

16 merits and a balance of hardships that tips sharply towards the plaintiff can support

17 issuance of a preliminary injunction, so long as the plaintiff also shows that there is

18 a likelihood of irreparable injury and that the injunction is in the public interest."

19 (internal quotation marks and citation omitted)).

20

ORDER GRANTING IN PART PLAINTIFFS' MOTION FOR
PRELIMINARY INJUNCTION ~ 8

1   A preliminary injunction can either be prohibitory or mandatory. *Marlyn*

2 *Nutraceuticals, Inc. v. Mucos Pharma GmbH & Co.*, 571 F.3d 873, 878 (9th Cir.

3 2009). A prohibitory injunction preserves the status quo which is the "last,

4 uncontested status which preceded the pending controversy." *Id.* at 879. A

5 mandatory injunction "orders a responsible party to take action." *Id.* at 878.

6 Mandatory injunctions are disfavored and require a higher showing that the "facts

7 and law clearly favor the moving party." *Garcia v. Google*, 786 F.3d 733, 740 (9th

8 Cir. 2015).

9   Plaintiffs contend they are seeking a prohibitory injunction to maintain the

10 "status quo." ECF Nos. 3, 78. Plaintiffs seek an "order enjoining Defendants from

11 doing two things: (1) enforcing the 2023 REMS, and (2) changing the status quo to

12 make mifepristone less available in the Plaintiff States." ECF No. 60 at 19.

13 However, when addressing Defendants' argument that the 2023 REMS is less

14 restrictive than any prior REMS, Plaintiffs contend they "seek to enjoin the

15 application of *any* REMS, such that mifepristone can be prescribed just like the

16 20,000+ other drugs that don't have one." *Id.* at 10. At oral argument, Plaintiffs

17 maintain they seek a prohibitory injunction.

18   The status quo, i.e., the last uncontested status preceding the pending

19 controversy, were the REMS in place prior to the 2023 REMS. Considering the

20

ORDER GRANTING IN PART PLAINTIFFS' MOTION FOR
PRELIMINARY INJUNCTION ~ 9

1 conflicting requests, the Court will apply the prohibitory injunction standard to the

2 extent Plaintiffs seek to maintain the status quo.

3 **A. Likelihood of Success on the Merits**

4 Plaintiffs assert they are likely to succeed on the success of the merits of the

5 claim that the 2023 REMS violated the Administrative Procedures Act ("APA").

6 ECF No. 3 at 16–19. Defendants disagree and also contend that Plaintiffs lack

7 standing and have not exhausted their administrative remedies. ECF No. 51.

8 *1. Standing*

9 Plaintiffs brings suit on behalf of themselves and as *parens patriae* in

10 protecting the health and well-being of its residents. *See* ECF No. 35. Defendants

11 argue Plaintiffs lack standing where the federal government is the ultimate *parens*

12 *patriae* and the alleged economic interests are insufficient to establish standing.

13 ECF No. 51.

14 The APA provides a cause of action to any "person … adversely affected or

15 aggrieved by agency action." 5 U.S.C. § 702. A state qualifies as a "person"

16 within the meaning of the APA. *See Maryland Dep't of Human Res. v. Dep't of*

17 *Health & Human Servs.*, 763 F.2d 1441, 1445 n.1 (D.C. Cir. 1985). The APA

18 allows a person to challenge agency action under various statutes. *See Block v.*

19 *Cmty. Nutrition Inst.*, 467 U.S. 340, 345 (1984).

20 //

1   a. *Parens Patriae* Suit

2   A *parens patriae* lawsuit allows a state to sue in a representative capacity on

3   behalf of its citizens' interests. *Gov't of Manitoba v. Bernhardt*, 923 F.3d 173, 178

4   (D.C. Cir. 2019). In order to establish standing beyond Article III's minimum, the

5   State must assert a quasi-sovereign interest "apart from the interests of particular

6   private parties." *Alfred L. Snapp & Son, Inc. v. Puerto Rico, ex rel., Barez*, 458

7   U.S. 592, 607 (1982). A state has a quasi-sovereign interest "in the health and

8   well-being – both physical and economic – of its residents" and "in not being

9   discriminatorily denied its rightful status within the federal system." *Id.* at 607.

10 Courts look to "whether the injury is one that the State, if it could, would likely

11 attempt to address through its sovereign lawmaking powers." *Id.*

12   Under the *Mellon* bar, a state lacks standing as *parens patriae* to bring an

13 action against the federal government. *Massachusetts v. Mellon*, 262 U.S. 447,

14 485–86 (1923). However, "courts must dispense with [the *Mellon* bar] if Congress

15 so provides." *Maryland People's Couns. v. FERC*, 760 F.2d 318, 321 (D.C. Cir.

16 1985). "The cases on the standing of states to sue the federal government seem to

17 depend on the kind of claim that the state advances. The decisions … are hard to

18 reconcile." *Arizona State Legislature v. Arizona Indep. Redistricting Comm'n*, 576

19 U.S. 787, 802, n.10 (2015).

20

ORDER GRANTING IN PART PLAINTIFFS' MOTION FOR
PRELIMINARY INJUNCTION ~ 11

1   Courts have determined that the APA alone does not demonstrate

2   congressional intent to authorize a state to sue the federal government as *parens*

3   *patriae*. *See Bernhardt*, 923 F.3d at 181; *Am. Fed'n of Tchrs. v. Cardona*, No.

4   5:20-CV-00455-EJD, 2021 WL 4461187, at *5 (N.D. Cal. Sept. 29, 2021).

5   However, states are not necessarily precluded from bringing a *parens patriae* suit

6   against the federal government, including where the underlying statute forming the

7   basis for the APA action authorizes a *parens patriae* suit. *See New York v. United*

8   *States Dep't of Lab.*, 477 F. Supp. 3d 1, 9, n.6 (S.D.N.Y. 2020); *New York v.*

9   *Biden*, No. 20-CV-2340(EGS), 2022 WL 5241880, at *7 (D.D.C. Oct. 6, 2022)

10   (allowing *parens patriae* suit against federal government where "Plaintiffs' efforts

11   to mitigate the spread of COVID-19 are aimed at protecting the public health of

12   their respective jurisdictions as a whole."); *Louisiana v. Becerra*, No. 3:21-CV-

13   04370, 2022 WL 4370448, at *5 (W.D. La. Sept. 21, 2022) (finding states have

14   *parens patriae* and/or quasi-sovereign interest in APA claims on behalf of

15   citizens).

16   Regardless of whether Plaintiffs have standing to assert claims on behalf of

17   its citizens under the APA in this case, Plaintiffs allege direct injuries sufficient to

18   confer standing. Therefore, the Court declines to resolve the *parens patriae* issue.

19   //

20   //

ORDER GRANTING IN PART PLAINTIFFS' MOTION FOR
PRELIMINARY INJUNCTION ~ 12

b. Direct Suit

In a direct suit where a state seeks redress for its own injuries, the state must meet Article III's minimum requirements. *Bernhardt*, 923 F.3d at 178. A plaintiff "must allege that they have suffered, or will imminently suffer, a 'concrete and particularized' injury in fact." *City & Cnty. of San Francisco v. United States Citizenship & Immigr. Servs.*, 981 F.3d 742, 754 (9th Cir. 2020) (quoting *Lujan v. Defs. of Wildlife*, 504 U.S. 555, 560 (1992)).

Under the APA, a claimant must also establish that their interests are "arguably within the zone of interests to be protected or regulated by the statute." *Match-E-Be-Nash-She-Wish Band of Pottawatomi Indians v. Patchak*, 567 U.S. 209, 224 (2012) (quoting *Ass'n of Data Processing Serv. Orgs., Inc. v. Camp*, 397 U.S. 150, 153 (1970)). This test is not "especially demanding" and requires only that the interest is "sufficiently congruent with those of the intended beneficiaries that the litigants are not more likely to frustrate than to further the statutory objectives." *City & Cnty. of San Francisco*, 981 F.3d at 755 (citations omitted).

Plaintiffs assert the following direct harm: (1) unrecoverable costs on the States' Medicaid and other state-funded health care programs from increased surgical abortions and pregnancy care, (2) practice restrictions on providers and pharmacists, including state employees, and (3) unrecoverable costs in implementing systems to comply with the 2023 REMS' patient agreement and

ORDER GRANTING IN PART PLAINTIFFS' MOTION FOR
PRELIMINARY INJUNCTION ~ 13

1 licensure requirements. ECF Nos. 3 at 29–30; 60 at 7–10 (citations to the record

2 omitted).

3   Plaintiffs have shown a reasonably probable threat to their economic

4 interests in the form of unrecoverable costs that are fairly traceable to the 2023

5 REMS, which are allegedly in violation of the APA. *See California v. Azar*, 911

6 F.3d 558, 571–73 (9th Cir. 2018) (finding state had standing due to economic

7 interests where state was responsible for reimbursing women who will seek

8 contraceptive care through state-run programs). Therefore, Plaintiffs have

9 established standing.

10   *2. Administrative Exhaustion*

11   Defendants contend Plaintiffs failed to exhaust their administrative remedies

12 by not filing a citizen petition under the 2023 REMS. ECF No. 51 at 14–19.

13 Plaintiffs maintain that a new citizen petition would be futile where FDA had the

14 same information and arguments prior to the January 2023 REMS decision. ECF

15 No. 60 at 4–7.

16   Under the APA, "[a] person suffering legal wrong because of agency action,

17 or adversely affected or aggrieved by agency action within the meaning of a

18 relevant statute, is entitled to judicial review thereof." 5 U.S.C. § 702. However,

19 the APA requires a plaintiff to "exhaust available administrative remedies before

20 bringing their grievances to federal court." *Idaho Sporting Congress, Inc. v.*

ORDER GRANTING IN PART PLAINTIFFS' MOTION FOR
PRELIMINARY INJUNCTION ~ 14

1   *Rittenhouse*, 305 F.3d 957, 965 (9th Cir. 2002) (citing 5 U.S.C. § 704).

2   Administrative exhaustion allows "the administrative agency in question to

3   exercise its expertise over the subject matter and to permit the agency an

4   opportunity to correct any mistakes that may have occurred during the proceeding,

5   thus avoiding unnecessary or premature judicial intervention into the

6   administrative process." *Buckingham v. Secretary of U.S. Dept. of Agr.*, 603 F.3d

7   1073, 1080 (9th Cir. 2020) (internal citation omitted). While the APA does not

8   mandate a process by which a plaintiff must exhaust remedies, the APA provides

9   for exhaustion "to the extent that it is required by statute or by agency rule as a

10   prerequisite to judicial review." *Darby v. Cisneros*, 509 U.S. 137, 153 (1993).

11   As relevant here, the FDA created a regulatory mechanism by which

12   interested persons may challenge agency activities under the Food, Drug, and

13   Cosmetic Act ("FDCA"). *See* 21 C.F.R. §§ 10.1(a), 10.25(a), 10.45(b). "An

14   interested person may petition the Commissioner to issue, amend, or revoke a

15   regulation or order, or to take or refrain from taking any other form of

16   administrative action …. in the form of a citizen petition." 21 C.F.R. § 10.25(a).

17   "A request that the Commissioner take … administrative action must first be the

18   subject of a final administrative decision based upon a petition submitted under

19   § 10.25(a) … before any legal action is filed in a court complaining of the action or

20   failure to act." 21 C.F.R. § 10.45(b). The purpose of administrative exhaustion is

ORDER GRANTING IN PART PLAINTIFFS' MOTION FOR
PRELIMINARY INJUNCTION ~ 15

1 to prevent "premature interference with agency processes, so that the agency may

2 function efficiently and so that it may have an opportunity to correct its own errors,

3 to afford the parties and the courts the benefit of its experience and expertise, and

4 to compile a record which is adequate for judicial review." *Tamosaitis v. URS*

5 *Inc.*, 781 F.3d 468, 478 (9th Cir. 2017).

6   Under exceptional circumstances, administrative exhaustion of an APA

7 claim is not required. *See Anderson v. Babbitt*, 230 F.3d 1158, 1164 (9th Cir.

8 2000). Exceptional circumstances include where there is "objective and

9 undisputed evidence" of administrative bias rendering pursuit of an administrative

10 remedy futile. *Id.* (brackets omitted); *see also SAIF Corp./Oregon Ship v.*

11 *Johnson*, 908 F.2d 1434, 1441 (9th Cir. 1990). Thus, where it appears the

12 agency's position is "already set" and it is "very likely" what the result would be,

13 such recourse is futile. *El Rescate Legal Servs., Inc. v. Exec. Off. of Immigr. Rev.*,

14 959 F.2d 742, 747 (9th Cir. 1991) (citation omitted); *see also Chinook Indian*

15 *Nation v. Zinke*, 326 F. Supp. 3d 1128, 1144 (W.D. Wash. 2018) ("There is

16 virtually no chance that requiring Plaintiffs to go through [agency's] formal request

17 process will make any difference.").

18   In 2020, fifteen Plaintiff States asked FDA to eliminate the REMS patient

19 agreement and certification requirements as "onerous and medically unnecessary"

20 and received a form response from FDA. ECF No. 60 at 5. In 2021, FDA

ORDER GRANTING IN PART PLAINTIFFS' MOTION FOR
PRELIMINARY INJUNCTION ~ 16

1 conducted a "full review" of REMS, including information about comparator drugs

2 with mifepristone. ECF No. 60 at 7. In 2022, the ACOG and other medical and

3 professional healthcare access organizations petitioned FDA to, in part, eliminate

4 the REMS as medically unnecessary and unduly burdensome for uses of

5 mifepristone, primarily for miscarriage management. ECF Nos. 35 at 47, ¶ 139; 60

6 at 4; 61-1. FDA rejected ACOG's citizen petition. ECF No. 35 at 51, ¶ 144.

7   Based on the information and requests already put forth before FDA, FDA

8 cannot credibly argue that its decision on the Mifepristone REMS Program would

9 change upon another citizen petition. *See, e.g.*, ECF Nos. 51-5 at 22–23 (assessing

10 whether to retain Mifeprex REMS); 61-13 at 2 (chronology of FDA

11 communications). Thus, the Court finds that administrative exhaustion through a

12 citizen petition on the January 2023 REMS would be futile.

13   *3. APA Claim*

14   Plaintiffs assert they are likely to succeed on the merits of the claim that the

15 2023 REMS is contrary to law and arbitrary and capricious under the APA. ECF

16 No. 3 at 19–29.

17   To obtain injunctive relief, Plaintiff must show that there are "serious

18 questions going to the merits" of its claims or that it is "likely to succeed on the

19 merits." *Cottrell*, 632 F.3d at 1131; *Farris*, 677 F.3d at 865. Under the APA, a

20 court shall "hold unlawful and set aside agency action, findings, and conclusions

ORDER GRANTING IN PART PLAINTIFFS' MOTION FOR
PRELIMINARY INJUNCTION ~ 17

1   found to be … arbitrary [and] capricious … or otherwise not in accordance with

2   law [or] in excess of statutory … authority, or limitations." 5 U.S.C. § 706(2)(A),

3   (C). Courts must uphold an agency action unless it (1) "relied on factors which

4   Congress has not intended it to consider," (2) "entirely failed to consider an

5   important aspect of the problem," (3) "offered an explanation for its decision that

6   runs counter to the evidence before the agency," or (4) the "decision is so

7   implausible that it could not be ascribed to a difference in view or the product of

8   agency expertise." *Turtle Island Restoration Network v. U.S. Dep't of Commerce*,

9   878 F.3d 725, 732–33 (9th Cir. 2017) (internal quotation marks omitted).

10 Additionally, a decision is arbitrary and capricious if it is internally inconsistent

11 with the underlying analysis. *Nat'l Parks Conservation Ass'n v. EPA*, 788 F.3d

12 1134, 1141 (9th Cir. 2015). Review is "at its most deferential" regarding an

13 agency's scientific determinations within its area of expertise. *Baltimore Gas &*

14 *Elec., Co. v. Nat. Res. Def. Council, Inc.*, 462 U.S. 87, 103 (1982).

15   Regulations are valid if they are "consistent with the statute under which

16 they are promulgated." *United States v. Larionoff*, 431 U.S. 864, 873 (1977).

17 Under the FDCA, a new drug cannot be marketed and prescribed until it undergoes

18 a rigorous approval process to determine that it is safe and effective. 21 U.S.C. §

19 355. For certain drugs, a risk evaluation and mitigation strategy (REMS) is

20 required when the agency determines, after considering six factors, it is "necessary

ORDER GRANTING IN PART PLAINTIFFS' MOTION FOR
PRELIMINARY INJUNCTION ~ 18

to ensure that the benefits of the drug outweigh the risks of the drug." 21 U.S.C. §

355-1(a)(1). An existing REMS may be modified or removed to "ensure the

benefits of the drug outweighs the risks of the drug [or] minimize the burden on the

health care delivery system of complying with the strategy." 21 U.S.C. § 355-

1(g)(4)(B).

Moreover, a REMS may include elements that are necessary to assure safe

use [ETASU] due to a drug's "inherent toxicity or potential harmfulness" if the

drug has "been shown to be effective, but is associated with a serious adverse drug

experience, can be approved only if, or would be withdrawn unless, such elements

are required as part of such strategy to mitigate a specific serious risk listed in the

labeling of the drug." 21 U.S.C. § 355-1(f)(1)(A). A "serious adverse drug

experience" is one that results in:

> death; an adverse drug experience that places the patient at immediate
> risk of death...; inpatient hospitalization or prolongation of existing
> hospitalization; a persistent or significant incapacity or substantial
> disruption of the ability to conduct normal life functions; or a
> congenital anomaly or birth defect; or based on appropriate medical
> judgment, may jeopardize the patient and may require a medical or
> surgical intervention to prevent [such] an outcome.

21 U.S.C. § 355-1(b)(4)(A).

If the FDA determines ETASU is required, the ETASU shall:

//

//

ORDER GRANTING IN PART PLAINTIFFS' MOTION FOR
PRELIMINARY INJUNCTION ~ 19

not be unduly burdensome on patient access to the drug, considering in particular – patients with serious or life-threatening diseases or conditions; patient who have difficulty accessing health care (such as patients in rural or medically underserved areas); and patients with functional limitations; and to the extent practicable, so as to minimize the burden on the health care delivery system – conform with [ETASU] for other drugs with similar, serious risks; and be designed to be compatible with established distribution, procurement, and dispensing systems from drugs.

21 U.S.C. § 355-1(f)(2)(C)–(D).

Plaintiffs contend that mifepristone no longer requires a REMS program with ETASU. ECF Nos. 3 at 19–21, 23–24; 60 at 11. Plaintiffs assert that (1) FDA acknowledges that serious adverse events are "exceedingly rare", (2) mifepristone's associated fatality rate is .00005%, with not a single death "casually attributed to mifepristone"(3) "all the data shows the mifepristone is among the safest drugs in the world, and safer than the vast majority of drugs for which FDA has never attempted to impose a REMS", and (4) "there is no reasoned scientific basis for subjecting it to additional burdens that are not applied to other, riskier medications." *See id.* Defendants do not address whether mifepristone qualifies for ETASU, asserting it need only determine whether modifications are appropriate under 21 U.S.C. § 355-1(g)(4)(B). *See* ECF Nos. 51 at 25; 78 at 22.

The FDA may modify or remove an approved REMS, including ETASU, if it determines "1 or more goals or elements should be … modified, or removed from the approved strategy [in part] to ensure the benefits of the drug outweigh the

1 risks of the drug." 21 U.S.C. § 355-1(g)(4)(B). Implicit in this assessment is

2 whether the drug's risks require REMS and/or ETASU. 21 U.S.C. § 355-1(a)(1),

3 (f)(1). Thus, it would be contrary to the plain language of the statute that the

4 agency need not consider arguments that mifepristone's REMS and ETASU should

5 be removed in whole or part based on criteria under 21 U.S.C. § 355-1(a)(1), (f)(1).

6   It is not the Court's role to review the scientific evidence and decide whether

7 mifepristone's benefits outweigh its risks without REMS and/or ETASU. That is

8 precisely FDA's role. However, based on the present record, FDA did not assess

9 whether mifepristone qualifies for REMS and ETASU based on the criteria set

10 forth under 21 U.S.C. § 355-1(a)(1), (f)(1). *See* ECF No. 51-4. Even under a

11 deferential review, it appears FDA failed to consider an important aspect of the

12 problem. *Turtle Island*, 878 F.3d at 732. Moreover, the record demonstrates

13 potentially internally inconsistent FDA findings regarding mifepristone's safety

14 profile. *Nat'l Parks Conservation*, 788 F.3d at 1141; *see, e.g.*, ECF Nos. 51-5 at

15 8–9 ("Serious adverse events … are rare" [and] mifepristone "is safe and effective

16 through 70 days gestation."); 51-9 (approving mifepristone for Cushing's

17 syndrome without a REMS considering risks of fetal loss).

18   Therefore, the Court finds there are serious issues going to the merits of

19 Plaintiffs' APA claims. *Cottrell*, 632 F.3d at 1131. The Court emphasizes this

20 finding is not binding at a trial on the merits. *Univ. of Texas v. Camenisch*, 451

ORDER GRANTING IN PART PLAINTIFFS' MOTION FOR
PRELIMINARY INJUNCTION ~ 21

1 U.S. 390, 395 (1981). Given this determination, the Court finds it unnecessary to

2 address the other arguments regarding the individual ETASU currently in place.

3 *See* ECF No. 3 at 21.

4 **B. Irreparable Harm**

5   Plaintiffs assert they will suffer irreparable harm from the 2023 REMS in at

6 least three ways: (1) financial costs on Plaintiffs that cannot be compensated, (2)

7 burdens on Plaintiffs' institutions and providers who provide abortion care, and (3)

8 harm to the health and well-being of patients and providers "by aggravating the

9 ongoing crisis of reduced access to abortion care." ECF No. 3 at 29.

10   A plaintiff seeking injunctive relief must "demonstrate that irreparable injury

11 is *likely* in the absence of an injunction." *Winter*, 555 U.S. at 22 (emphasis in

12 original). "Issuing a preliminary injunction based only on a possibility of

13 irreparable harm is inconsistent with [the Supreme Court's] characterization of

14 injunctive relief as an extraordinary remedy that may only be awarded upon a clear

15 showing that the plaintiff is entitled to such relief." *Id.* "Irreparable harm is

16 traditionally defined as harm for which there is no adequate legal remedy, such as

17 an award of damages." *Arizona Dream Act Coalition v. Brewer*, 757 F.3d 1053,

18 1068 (9th Cir. 2014). A court may imply a lack of irreparable harm where there is

19 no "speedy action" and a plaintiff sleeps on its rights. *Lydo Enters. v. City of Las*

20 *Vegas*, 745 F.2d 1211, 1213 (9th Cir. 1984).

ORDER GRANTING IN PART PLAINTIFFS' MOTION FOR
PRELIMINARY INJUNCTION ~ 22

1   Plaintiffs assert that the Mifepristone REMS Program imposes costs that are

2 not compensable where the restriction of access to mifepristone causes patients to

3 miss the window for medication abortion, leaving patients with procedural abortion

4 or carrying a pregnancy to term, options that impose higher costs on Plaintiffs'

5 state-run health care programs. ECF No. 3 at 29–30. Plaintiffs also contend the

6 ongoing implementation of the 2023 REMS modifications impose costs on

7 Plaintiffs. *Id.* at 33. Economic costs that may not be recovered through the

8 ordinary course of litigation satisfy the irreparable harm standard. *Idaho v. Coeur*

9 *d'Alene Tribe*, 794 F.3d 1039, 1046 (9th Cir. 2015); *see also California v. U.S.*

10 *Health & Human Servs.*, 390 F. Supp. 3d 1061, 1065 (N.D. Cal. 2019). The Court

11 finds that the alleged unrecoverable economic costs in this case is sufficient to

12 demonstrate irreparable harm. The Court need not reach Plaintiffs' other bases of

13 irreparable harm.

14   Defendants argue Plaintiffs fail to show irreparable harm on two grounds:

15 (1) the 2023 REMS loosen restrictions and (2) Plaintiffs delayed in filing this

16 action. ECF No. 51 at 30. First, even taking Defendants' argument that the "net

17 effect" of the 2023 REMS lessens restrictions, Plaintiffs continue to assert that *no*

18 restrictions are necessary and the 2023 REMS impose new restrictions that

19 Plaintiffs are still working to implement. *See* ECF No. 3 at 33. Second, as to any

20 delay, Plaintiffs contend they did not know FDA would approve the 2023 REMS

ORDER GRANTING IN PART PLAINTIFFS' MOTION FOR
PRELIMINARY INJUNCTION ~ 23

1   in light of the *Dobbs* decision[2] until January 2023. ECF No. 60 at 15–16; *see also*

2   ECF No. 78 at 9. This is a complex case with 18 Plaintiffs. The Court finds

3   Plaintiffs' less than two-month delay from the FDA approval minimal considering

4   the record and issues in this case. *Lydo*, 745 F.2d at 1213. Accordingly, these are

5   not bases to deny preliminary relief based on the lack of irreparable harm.

6   Plaintiffs have satisfied this element.

7   **C. Balancing of Equities and Public Interest**

8   Plaintiffs assert that the equities and public interest weigh strongly in their

9   favor where the public's health is at stake. ECF No. 3 at 36.

10   When the government is a party to a case in which a preliminary injunction

11   is sought, the balance of the equities and public interest factors merge. *Drakes Bay*

12   *Oyster Co. v. Jewell*, 747 F.3d 1073, 1092 (9th Cir. 2014). The public's interest in

13   health care favors a preliminary injunction where the agency's action likely

14   "results in worse health outcomes." *New York v. U.S. Dep't of Homeland Sec.*, 969

15   F.3d 42, 87 (2d Cir. 2020).

16   Plaintiffs contend the public has an interest in access to safe and effective

17   medicine for those who terminate their pregnancies. ECF No. 3 at 36. Defendants

18   contend the public interest is "best served by deferring to FDA's judgments about

19

20   ---

    [2]   *Dobbs v. Jackson Women's Health Org.*, 142 S. Ct. 2228 (2022).

ORDER GRANTING IN PART PLAINTIFFS' MOTION FOR
PRELIMINARY INJUNCTION ~ 24

1   what restrictions are necessary to ensure drugs are safe." ECF No. 51 at 32. The

2   Court agrees with this general premise, but the allegations in this case are that FDA

3   made findings (or failed to make findings) that the Court does not defer to, i.e.

4   those contrary to law and those that are arbitrary and capricious. Thus, this

5   argument does not strongly favor Defendants. Based on the public health and

6   administrative considerations at issue in this case, Plaintiffs have shown the

7   balance of the equities sharply tip in their favor and the public interest favors a

8   preliminary injunction.

9   The Court finds Plaintiffs have satisfied the "alternative" *Cottrell* test. At

10   this point, the Court will issue a status quo preliminary injunction but not a

11   mandatory preliminary injunction.

12   **D. Relief**

13   The Court turns to Plaintiffs' remedy. Defendants contend that Plaintiffs'

14   requested relief exceeds any permissible scope where Plaintiffs seek an order

15   enjoining "any action to remove mifepristone from the market or otherwise cause

16   the drug to become less available." ECF No. 51 at 33–36. Plaintiffs counter that

17   an order enjoining Defendants from the following is appropriate: "(1) enforcing the

18   2023 REMS, and (2) changing the status quo to make mifepristone less available in

19   the Plaintiff States." ECF No. 60 at 19.

20   //

1   *1. Type of Relief*

2   When the Court determines a preliminary injunction is warranted,

3   "injunctive relief should be no more burdensome to the defendant than necessary

4   to provide complete relief to the plaintiffs." *Califano v. Yamasaki*, 442 U.S. 682,

5   702 (1979). "The purpose of such interim equitable relief is not to conclusively

6   determine the rights of the parties but to balance the equities as the litigation

7   moves forward." *California v. Azar*, 911 F.3d 558, 582 (9th Cir. 2018). In

8   crafting a remedy, courts "need not grant the total relief sought by the applicant but

9   may mold its decree to meet the exigencies of the particular case." *Trump v. Int'l*

10   *Refugee Assistance Project*, 137 S. Ct. 2080, 2087 (2017) (citation omitted).

11   "Ordinarily when a regulation is not promulgated in compliance with the

12   APA, the regulation is invalid." *Paulsen v. Daniels*, 413 F.3d 999, 1008 (9th Cir.

13   2005) (citation omitted). "The effect of invalidating an agency rule is to reinstate

14   the rule previously in force." *Id.* (citation omitted). "The scope of an injunction is

15   within the broad discretion of the district court." *TrafficSchool.com, Inc. v.*

16   *Edriver Inc.*, 653 F.3d 820, 829 (9th Cir. 2011).

17   First, the relief Plaintiffs seek by enjoining FDA from enforcing REMS is

18   inconsistent. *Compare* ECF Nos. 3 at 37 (enjoining 2023 REMS) *with* 3-1 at 3

19   (enjoining REMS entirely). Enjoining REMS from mifepristone entirely is well

20   beyond the status quo. Indeed, enjoining the 2023 REMS and returning to the

1 status quo would eliminate the ability of pharmacies to provide the drug, thereby

2 reducing its availability. This runs directly counter to Plaintiffs' request.

3   Second, the relief Plaintiffs seek by enjoining FDA from reducing

4 mifepristone's availability does not exceed the permissible scope of relief. In

5 preserving the status quo, it is fair and equitable for FDA to not act with respect to

6 the Mifepristone REMS Program until a determination is made on the merits. *See*

7 *Boardman v. Pac. Seafood Grp.*, 822 F.3d 1011, 1024 (9th Cir. 2016) (finding

8 court's prohibition on taking any further action "effectively preserved the parties'

9 last uncontested status"); *Bracco Diagnostics, Inc. v. Shalala*, 963 F. Supp. 20, 30

10 (D.D.C. 1997) (enjoining "FDA from proceeding with any approval or review

11 proceedings"). This is consistent with the APA authorizing courts to stay agency

12 action "to preserve status or rights pending conclusion of the review proceedings."

13 5 U.S.C. § 705.

14   Accordingly, Defendants are preliminary enjoined from altering the status or

15 rights of the parties under the operative Mifepristone REMS Program until a

16 determination on the merits.

17   *2. Scope of Relief*

18   As a final matter, the Court notes Plaintiffs appear to seek a nationwide

19 injunction. *See* ECF No. 3-1.

20

ORDER GRANTING IN PART PLAINTIFFS' MOTION FOR
PRELIMINARY INJUNCTION ~ 27

1   Generally, there is no "requirement that an injunction affect only the parties

2 in the suit." *Bresgal v. Brock*, 843 F.2d 1163, 1169 (9th Cir. 1987). While courts

3 have the authority to issue nationwide preliminary injunctions, the Ninth Circuit

4 cautions they are for "exceptional cases" and that have proof of "an articulated

5 connection to a plaintiff's particular harm." *E. Bay Sanctuary Covenant v. Barr*,

6 934 F.3d 1026, 1029 (9th Cir. 2019). "District judges must require a showing of

7 nationwide impact or sufficient similarity to the plaintiff states to foreclose

8 litigation in other districts." *Azar*, 911 F.3d at 584; *see also City & Cnty. of San*

9 *Francisco v. Trump*, 897 F.3d 1225, 1244 (9th Cir. 2018) (noting record must be

10 developed on nationwide impact).

11   First, the Court finds a nationwide injunction inappropriate where the record

12 does not demonstrate a nationwide impact of sufficient similarity to Plaintiffs'

13 situation. *Azar*, 911 F.3d at 584. Abortion restrictions vary state-by-state and

14 Plaintiffs allege harm not shared nationwide. For example, Plaintiffs allege harm

15 from the 2023 REMS in light of the influx of patients from states who do not have

16 similar services available. Second, the Court finds a nationwide injunction

17 inappropriate where there is the potential for competing litigation.[3] *Id.* at 583

18 _____

19 [3]   *See, e.g., All. For Hippocratic Med. v. FDA*, No. 2:22-cv-00223-Z (N.D.

20 Tex. Jan. 13, 2023).

ORDER GRANTING IN PART PLAINTIFFS' MOTION FOR
PRELIMINARY INJUNCTION ~ 28

1   (noting courts should consider "the equities of non-parties who are deprived the

2   right to litigate in other forums.").

3   Under these circumstances, the Court declines to issue a nationwide

4   injunction and will enter the preliminary injunction as it applies to Plaintiff States.

5   **II.   Amici Briefs**

6   The Court has broad discretion to grant or refuse a prospective amicus

7   participation. *See Hoptowit v. Ray*, 682 F.2d 1237, 1260 (9th Cir. 1982),

8   *abrogated on other grounds by Sandin v. Conner*, 515 U.S. 472 (1995). Amicus

9   may be either impartial individuals or interested parties. *See Funbus Sys., Inc. v.*

10 *Cal. Pub. Utils. Comm'n*, 801 F.2d 1120, 1125 (9th Cir. 1986). In deciding

11 whether to grant leave to file an amicus brief, courts should consider whether the

12 briefing "supplement[s] the efforts of counsel, and draw[s] the court's attention to

13 law that escaped consideration." *Miller-Wohl Co., Inc. v. Comm'r of Labor &*

14 *Indus. Mont.*, 694 F.2d 203, 204 (9th Cir. 1982). "An amicus brief should

15 normally be allowed when . . . the amicus has an interest in some other case that

16 may be affected by the decision in the present case, or when the amicus has unique

17 information or perspective that can help the court beyond the help that the lawyers

18 for the parties are able to provide. . . . Otherwise, leave to file an amicus curiae

19 brief should be denied." *Cmty. Ass'n for Restoration of Env't (CARE) v. DeRuyter*

20

ORDER GRANTING IN PART PLAINTIFFS' MOTION FOR
PRELIMINARY INJUNCTION ~ 29

1 *Bros. Dairy*, 54 F. Supp. 2d 974, 975 (E.D. Wash. 1999) (internal citations

2 omitted).

3   While these motions are unopposed, the proposed briefs offer no additional

4 legal or substantive information that is particularly helpful to the Court's findings

5 on the present motion. The briefs may be more useful during a trial on the merits.

6 Therefore, the motions are denied.

7 **ACCORDINGLY, IT IS HEREBY ORDERED:**

8   1. Plaintiffs' Motion for Preliminary Injunction (ECF No. 3) is **GRANTED**

9   **in part**.

10   2. Pursuant to Federal Rule of Civil Procedure 65(a), Defendants and their

11   officers, agents, servants, employees, attorneys, and any person in active

12   concert or participation, are **PRELIMINARILY ENJOINED** from:

13   "altering the status quo and rights as it relates to the availability of

14   Mifepristone under the current operative January 2023 Risk

15   Evaluation and Mitigation Strategy under 21 U.S.C. § 355-1 in

16   Plaintiff States."

17   3. No bond shall be required. Fed. R. Civ. P. 65(c).

18   4. Third Parties' Unopposed Motion for Leave to File Amicus Curiae Brief

19   (ECF No. 52) is **DENIED.**

20

ORDER GRANTING IN PART PLAINTIFFS' MOTION FOR
PRELIMINARY INJUNCTION ~ 30

1   5. Third Parties' Unopposed Motion for Leave to File Amicus Brief (ECF

2   No. 69) is **DENIED**.

3   The District Court Executive is directed to enter this Order and furnish

4 copies to counsel.

5   DATED April 7, 2023.

7   THOMAS O. RICE
                   United States District Judge

ORDER GRANTING IN PART PLAINTIFFS' MOTION FOR
PRELIMINARY INJUNCTION ~ 31